TABLE OF CONTENTS

Unless otherwise indicated, all Scripture quotations are taken from the King James Version of the Bible.
The Covenant of 58 Blessings
ISBN 1-56394-011-6/B-47
Copyright © 1994 by **MIKE MURDOCK**
All publishing rights belong exclusively to Wisdom International
Publisher/Editor: Deborah Murdock Johnson
Published by The Wisdom Center · 4051 Denton Hwy. · Ft. Worth, Texas 76117
1-817-759-BOOK · 1-817-759-0300
You Will Love Our Website...! www.TheWisdomCenter.tv

Accuracy Department: To our Friends and Partners...We welcome any comments on errors or misprints you find in our book...Email our department: AccuracyDept@thewisdomcenter.tv. Your aid in helping us excel is highly valued.

DEDICATION TO MY PARTNERS

You Listened...When I shared my illogical and odd experiences.

You Believed...When I pointed to the Covenant given to us.

You Explored...When I gave you a chance to use your faith experimentally in sowing a specific Seed and giving it an Assignment.

You Stretched...When I asked you to use your faith.

You Sowed...When I challenged you to follow me in sowing a Seed into the work of God.

You Tasted...The unbelievable rewards of the Harvest promised by the Lord of the Harvest.

You Wait Expectantly...For the completion of the Promise of the 100-fold return in Mark 10:28-30.

"For My thoughts are not your thoughts, neither are your ways My ways, saith the Lord. For as the heavens are higher than the earth, so are My ways higher than your ways, and My thoughts than your thoughts," (Isaiah 55:8-9).

"Believe in the Lord your God, so shall ye be established; believe His prophets, so shall ye prosper," (2 Chronicles 20:20).

MY PERSONAL TESTIMONY
(Why I Wrote This Book)

━━━━━➤❦⋘━━━━━

A number of years ago, I was sitting in an airport in Tulsa, Oklahoma, waiting for bad weather to subside. Every airline had been cancelled for eight hours. Remembering an idea I had carried for some time, I pulled out my black legal pad notebook and proceeded to write down every Scripture from Genesis through Revelation that contained some kind of blessing or promise. My goal was to create a book without any other Scripture except the blessing Scriptures...in the sequence that they were recorded in the Bible. It would reveal the stream of blessing that God had created to flow into mankind...in every single book of the Bible. At that time, it never occurred to me to see exactly how many kinds of blessings were obvious.

That book later became known as the best selling, "The Blessing Book." Tens of thousands were sold through other ministries.

Approximately two years later, I sat on a platform in Washington, DC. My pastor friend was receiving the church tithe and offerings. As I was sitting there, contemplating the amount I should sow, The Holy Spirit very gently nudged me with a question, "How many kinds of blessings are there in My Word?" I remembered my special study. "58," I replied inside my spirit. (Now, there's probably a lot more than 58, but that's how many I counted personally.)

"Plant a special Seed of $58 into this offering today. It will become a memory in the mind of God and will be a monument to your faith that you want to stand in covenant with your God for the entire 58 blessings to occur during your lifetime."

It sounded utterly ridiculous to me. Nobody heard it. It was so strong, I remember looking around and wondering if anybody had felt or sensed what was going on inside me.

I have always known that certain numbers were important to God. He is always specific. Always illogical. Whether it is dealing with Gideon's 300...or instructing the Israelites to walk around the walls of Jericho seven consecutive days...and seven times around the walls on the seventh day...or the prophet telling the leper to dip seven times in Jordan. Numbers do matter. Obviously, they do not seem to matter to us...but to the One Who gave us the instruction.

I wrote out a special Seed for $58 immediately. Suddenly The Holy Spirit again whispered, "Plant a special Seed of $58 for your son, Jason. It will represent that you are in covenant—that I will honor your son and bless him in his life likewise."

Obviously, my mind began to dig for Scriptural validation. Was it my personal imagination? It never lingered long in my heart for that consideration as I lived continuously in relationship and communion with The Holy Spirit.

It does not take me long to recognize my mother's voice on the telephone.

Relationship really makes a difference.

That is why I never get into an argument with

people concerning whether God spoke to me or not. If He spoke to me, it does not make any difference whether they believe it or not.

I wrote out a second Seed-faith gift of $58 and this time I placed Jason's name on it specifically.

I believe that giving money as a trade out for a miracle borders on blasphemy. Just recently, I have had people throw down hundreds of dollars on a table asking me to pray a specific prayer of blessing over their life. I refused. Certainly, I could have used their offering for our ministry and it is very needed...but the spirit and motive behind it reminds me of Acts 8:18-23. "And when Simon saw that through the laying on of the apostles' hands the Holy Ghost was given, he offered them money, Saying, Give me also this power, that on whomsoever I lay hands, he may receive the Holy Ghost. But Peter said unto him, Thy money perish with thee, because thou hast thought that the gift of God may be purchased with money. Thou hast neither part nor lot in this matter: for thy heart is not right in the sight of God,...if perhaps the thought of thine heart may be forgiven thee. For I perceive that thou are in the gall of bitterness, and in the bond of iniquity."

My mind very carefully reviewed all that I could remember about giving offerings to the Lord. Was there an occasion in the Bible where a man specifically gave an offering to the Lord and experienced a direct result? Certainly. "And David built there an altar unto the Lord, and offered burnt offerings and peace offerings. So the Lord was intreated for the land, and the plague was stayed from Israel," (2 Samuel 24:25). This followed the horrible tragedy of 70,000 people dying within 72 hours following David's sin.

Scripturally, the purpose of sowing or giving to God is to create the rewards of obedience.

"Honour the Lord with thy substance, and with the firstfruits of thine increase: So shall thy barns be filled with plenty, and thy presses shall burst out with new wine," (Proverbs 3:9-10).

"Bring ye all the tithes into the storehouse, that there may be meat in Mine house, and prove Me now herewith, saith the Lord of hosts, if I will not open you the windows of heaven, and pour you out a blessing, that there shall not be room enough to receive it. And I will rebuke the devourer for your sakes, and he shall not destroy the fruits of your ground; neither shall your vine cast her fruit before the time in the field, saith the Lord of hosts. And all nations shall call you blessed," (Malachi 3:10-12).

"Give, and it shall be given unto you; good measure, pressed down, and shaken together, and running over, shall men give into your bosom. For with the same measure that you mete withal it shall be measured to you again," (Luke 6:38).

When Peter discussed leaving all to follow Jesus, Jesus answered and said, "Verily I say unto you, There is no man that hath left house, or brethren, or sisters, or father, or mother, or wife, or children, or lands, for My sake, and the gospel's, But he shall receive an hundredfold now in this time, houses, and brethren, and sisters, and mothers, and children, and lands, with persecutions; and in the world to come eternal life," (Mark 10:29-30).

It astounds me that men who want to believe so

many other Scriptures have a problem with these Scriptures. Those who believe what Jesus said about Heaven and hell are incensed that anyone would want to embrace these Scriptures on reward, Harvest, and financial response from God to a single act of Seed-sowing or an act of disobedience.

Some feel that it is sinful to expect a financial gift from God. Yet, every day these same individuals beg God for things far more valuable and far more worthy than money. They ask for Wisdom, the salvation of a loved one, the healing of an uncle who has cursed God his entire lifetime. They beg God to send someone to buy their house, or car, or even ask the Lord to win a lottery on which they have gambled.

People are funny. Maybe very blind.

Anyway, I've got to get back to my story.

I started believing about Jason after I planted the special Seed of $58 and gave it an Assignment— that God would remember my Seed as a testimony of my confidence toward Him regarding His covenant with me. My money was important to me. My faith was to God. My mind wandered that morning after I planted the Seed. I had gone through a very devastating divorce when my son was just 18 months old. There had been deep difficulties and walls of conflict as his mother had married two more times. Two child custody cases had left me broke. I had really given up on any possibility of having my son and being able to raise him in my presence and serving the Lord in church.

But, I had given my Seed an Assignment. You see, a watermelon seed contains an invisible instruction to create watermelons. An apple seed contains an invisible instruction to create apples. A tomato seed never consults a cantaloupe seed with a puzzled question, "What do you think I ought to become?" You see, the Creator of this universe places an instruction...an Assignment...in everything He creates. It may be invisible to the human eye. It may be a silent message or Assignment. But the Harvest reveals what it contains. That's why, with our Seeds that we sow into this world, it is important to give them invisible instructions and call in the Harvest where we need the results the most.

Within a few weeks, I landed back at the Dallas airport and was very surprised to see my secretary standing there. She had never met me in the airport to my knowledge.

"Jason will be here in one hour at the other airport, Love Field," she said excitedly.

"What's wrong?" I instantly was tense.

"Nothing," she said. "His mother has just decided that he can come spend the rest of his life with you."

That was the beginning of a most incredible journey of miracles that I have ever known during my whole lifetime.

One night, in a little Bible study in Dallas, I rather hesitatingly told the people about my experience with the $58 Seed. I suggested that they plant it as a special signal and message to the Lord that they were in covenant with Him for something specific with their life.

"You cannot buy a miracle with money," I insisted as I always do. "But, you can plant this as a Seed of your faith and believe God will provide a supernatural Harvest as He did for my life."

That night a couple wrote the name of their daughter on their check. She was addicted to cocaine. Her life was in shambles. They were devastated. Fourteen days later, that daughter accepted Christ and was set free from drugs.

One night, Jesse Perez, who traveled with me wherever I went, planted a special Seed of $58. He wrote on the left hand corner of his check, "Better family relations." You see, there was a sister who had left home 48 years prior. No one in the entire family had seen nor heard from her in those 48 years. No one knew whether she was alive or dead. He had not seen two of his daughters in five years. Jesse had not had a meal with his entire family for approximately 15 years. Fourteen days after he planted his Seed, he was able to spend several days with his two daughters. He got to experience a meal with his entire household and, within 90 days, they had located and found that sister unheard of for 48 years. His 86 year old father accepted Christ. His mother gave her life to the Lord and his sisters and his daughters had marvellous spiritual experiences with God—within days and weeks.

It would astound you if I had kept every single letter...recorded every single testimonial...and perhaps it's best that I have not, though my files are stacked full of incredible letters validating the power of God.

God wants to be worshiped...not His Seed that He provides for us.

Many ministers have asked me about the mystery of the $58 and the covenant with God.

I don't really have any answers. That's like

asking Naaman to analyze why dipping in Jordan removed his leprosy. It is like asking Joshua how the marching affected the walls of Jericho so that they fell approximately on the seventh day. It is like asking the blind man to explain the chemistry in the spittle and the clay that removed a lifetime of blindness.

I really don't know. I do speculate a lot. I crave Wisdom. I have an intense appetite to understand what creates currents of miracles.

My thoughts are that it is not the amount of the Seed that matters a whole lot to God. But, whether or not it is an act of faith. I feel that your Seed is what God multiplies...but your faith is why He multiplies it.

Some have sowed Seed with carnal motives to manipulate, gamble and simply experiment.

I doubt that they will ever see any results to their Seed. God cannot be bought with silver and gold.

Thousands have seen miracles. Unbelievable miracles.

I do believe that any miracle you ever receive from God will require an act of faith on your part. I also believe that you will have to believe some man of God...somewhere...sometime...before God ever releases a miracle toward you. "Believe in the Lord your God, so shall you be established; believe His prophets, so shall you prosper," (2 Chronicles 20:20).

People are cocky these days. Very arrogant toward preachers. They sneer and the world system will invest millions of dollars to wreck a man's credibility. Consequently, thousands of naive and unthinking sheep follow the pied piper of the media over the cliff into the abyss of doubt and unbelief.

Certainly, there are wolves in sheep's clothing.

Nobody can doubt that. But they will stand before their Maker to give an account for every idle word and every false manipulative system and program they have implemented.

14 Facts About Blessings

1.   **God Wants To Bless You In A Special Way.**

2.   **He Is Capable Of Providing Every One Of These 58 Kinds Of Blessings To Your Life And To Those You Love Every Day Of Your Life.**

3.   **You Must Do Something...Some Act Of Obedience Before You Will Experience Any Rewards For Your Obedience.**

4.   **He Will Often Ask You To Do Something Illogical, Impractical And Something Others Have Never Heard Of.**

5.   **He May Tell You To Do Something That He Never Speaks To Others To Do...Uniquely Your Personal Instruction, Because It Forces You To Use Your Faith.**

6.   **What He Tells You To Do May Be For You Alone And Not Others.**

7.   **He May Give An Instruction To A Man Of God Who Then Imparts That Instruction On To You Like He Did The Widow Of Zarephath Through Elijah The Prophet.**

8.   **You May Have To Go On The Prophet's Word Alone Instead Of Your Own Inner Confirmation Of The Spirit.** (This happened to the widow of Zarephath. It was the word of the prophet she believed.) I had an interesting experience in

Florida in a conference. A well-known man of God sent me a note along with other men of God around me saying he was supposed to address the conference. I never felt it whatsoever. Finally, his tears moved me and I gave him the microphone. The power of God fell through his ministry in an unprecedented way. Miracles happened all over the auditorium. I never felt the presence or moving of The Holy Spirit during the entire time that he ministered. Even when the service was over, I did not "feel" it whatsoever. God taught me something. He is moving around me whether I feel it or not. Wisdom permits others to honor The Holy Spirit moving within themselves.

9. If You Choose To Disobey An Instruction Of The Man Of God, You Must Live With The Consequences Or Losses Your Doubt Has Created.

10. If You Are Waiting For A Specific Instruction To Come From A Man Of God That Fits With Your Philosophy, Behavior Pattern, Or The Logic Of Your Mind...You May Live Your Entire Lifetime Without Ever Experiencing A Miracle.

11. When A Man Of God Gives You An Instruction, It Is Your Faith In God That Causes The Reward System To Work For You.

12. Your Reaction To A Man Of God Determines God's Reaction To You.

13. God Never Tells You To Do Something That Is Impossible, But Usually Illogical.

14. It Is Not Merely A Seed That We Sow (Of Our Time, Love, Money) But It Is Our Faith That Is Wrapped Around The Seed That Really

Produces The Harvest We Desire.

I really hope that when you finish reading this book, you will sit down and plant a very special Seed of $58 into the work of the Lord somewhere. It certainly does not have to be my own ministry. In fact, I would encourage you to plant it in your local church and pastor...wrapped with your intense faith in God and count off 58 days on your calendar. Then, document the unusual things that begin to happen for good in your life and those you love.

You will never be the same again.

Some people will misinterpret this grossly. It saddens me, but I cannot go another several years without sharing this and giving others access to a potential miracle.

Just a quick closing thought. My mother and father were well into their seventies. Financial rivers have never flowed at the Murdock household. In fact, the highest salary any church ever paid my father as pastor was $125 per week. My father had to pay his own house note, car, etc. Yes, seven children were in our family. Consequently, Mother and Daddy could never afford medical insurance. Especially, they could not begin it while they were in their seventies. Tragedy struck and my mother required a double bypass surgery in Houston, Texas at a major hospital. Upon leaving the hospital, they found that one of their major bills alone was $48,000 for the surgery. My poor parents scraped every cent they could possibly get together and eventually (with a little help from myself and other children) got the bill to $26,622.

God impressed me to record my story about the $58 Seed on a little cassette tape and send it to my parents and a few other friends. My mother called, "Son, Daddy and I felt God on that tape. We're sending a $58 Seed. We sure need some miracles at our house." I knew they did, too.

It was sort of funny, but my mother called me after one week and said, "Son, it's been a week now and I can't say that I've actually seen any miracles. Am I doing anything wrong?" I laughed aloud, and said, "Of course not, Mother. Give God time."

She did the same thing the following week. But, when I returned home from a meeting at the end of the third week, three messages were on my machine to call home. When my mother and father answered, they were both so excited they could hardly talk.

"Son, I can hardly catch my breath," said my father who rarely is that talkative. What happened? That hospital had written and called saying, "Your bill of $26,622 came to our attention. Once in a while, we want to do something that helps somebody. Your bill is marked, paid in full."

The hospital had paid my mother and father's entire remainder of that specific bill, $26,622.

Coincidence?

Well, what are the chances of it happening to you? What are the chances of it happening within 21 days from the time you plant a very illogical, impractical and ridiculous Seed of $58? No, I would not build my entire life on a coincidence...nor even a one time experience. My life is built on The Word of the living God. If I never received a Harvest, and I never saw a miracle resulting from any Seed I planted...I would still love my precious Jesus with all of my heart, serve God with total abandonment, and strive to tell people about Jesus throughout the world. He is what is important on earth, not a few stacks of money.

Please read my heart accurately. I am just saying that at some point in your life..."When you want something that you have never had, God will tell you to do something that you have never done."

That's when your journey of miracles will finally begin.

Mike Murdock

≈ 1 ≈

ABILITIES

And I have filled him with the spirit of God, in wisdom, and in understanding, and in knowledge, and in all manner of workmanship. *Exodus 31:3*

Having then gifts differing according to the grace that is given to us, whether prophecy, let us prophesy according to the proportion of faith. *Romans 12:6*

Now there are diversities of gifts, but the same Spirit. And there are differences of administrations, but the same Lord. And there are diversities of operations, but it is the same God which worketh all in all. But the manifestation of the Spirit is given to every man to profit withal. For to one is given by the Spirit the word of wisdom; to another the word of knowledge by the same Spirit; To another faith by the same Spirit; to another the gifts of healing by the same Spirit; To another the working of miracles; to another prophecy; to another discerning of spirits; to another divers kinds of tongues; to another the interpretation of tongues: But all these worketh that one and the selfsame Spirit, dividing to every man severally as He will. *1 Corinthians 12:4-11*

Who comforteth us in all our tribulation, that we may be able to comfort them which are in any trouble, by the comfort wherewith we ourselves are comforted of God. *2 Corinthians 1:4*

2

ABUNDANCE

For the Lord thy God blesseth thee, as He promised thee: and thou shalt lend unto many nations, but thou shalt not borrow; and thou shalt reign over many nations, but they shall not reign over thee. If there be among you a poor man of one of thy brethren within any of thy gates in thy land which the Lord thy God giveth thee, thou shalt not harden thine heart, nor shut thine hand from thy poor brother.

Deuteronomy 15:6-7

And the Lord thy God will make thee plenteous in every work of thine hand, in the fruit of thy body, and in the fruit of thy cattle, and in the fruit of thy land, for good: for the Lord will again rejoice over thee for good, as He rejoiced over thy fathers.

Deuteronomy 30:9

The righteous shall flourish like the palm tree: he shall grow like a cedar in Lebanon.   *Psalm 92:12*

I will open rivers in high places, and fountains in the midst of the valleys: I will make the wilderness a pool of water, and the dry land springs of water.

Isaiah 41:18

3

ANGELS

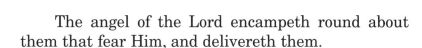

The angel of the Lord encampeth round about them that fear Him, and delivereth them.

Psalm 34:7

For He shall give His angels charge over thee, to keep thee in all thy ways. They shall bear thee up in their hands, lest thou dash thy foot against a stone.

Psalm 91:11-12

In all their affliction He was afflicted, and the angel of His presence saved them: in His love and in His pity He redeemed them; and He bare them, and carried them all the days of old.   *Isaiah 63:9*

Then the devil leaveth Him, and, behold, angels came and ministered unto Him.   *Matthew 4:11*

Take heed that ye despise not one of these little ones; for I say unto you, That in heaven their angels do always behold the face of My Father which is in heaven.   *Matthew 18:10*

Likewise, I say unto you, there is joy in the presence of the angels of God over one sinner that repenteth.   *Luke 15:10*

4

ASSURANCE

Sojourn in this land, and I will be with thee, and will bless thee; for unto thee, and unto thy seed, I will give all these countries, and I will perform the oath which I sware unto Abraham thy father. *Genesis 26:3*

I will seek that which was lost, and bring again that which was driven away, and will bind up that which was broken, and will strengthen that which was sick: but I will destroy the fat and the strong; I will feed them with judgment. *Ezekiel 34:16*

I will not leave you comfortless: I will come to you. *John 14:18*

And we know that all things work together for good to them that love God, to them who are the called according to His purpose. *Romans 8:28*

Wherein God, willing more abundantly to shew unto the heirs of promise the immutability of His counsel, confirmed it by an oath: That by two immutable things, in which it was impossible for God to lie, we might have a strong consolation, who have fled for refuge to lay hold upon the hope set before us. *Hebrews 6:17-18*

So that we may boldly say, The Lord is my helper, and I will not fear what man shall do unto me. *Hebrews 13:6*

5

AUTHORITY

So God created man in His own image, in the image of God created He him; male and female created He them. And God blessed them, and God said unto them, Be fruitful, and multiply, and replenish the earth, and subdue it: and have dominion over the fish of the sea, and over the fowl of the air, and over every living thing that moveth upon the earth.

Genesis 1:27-28

And the fear of you and the dread of you shall be upon every beast of the earth, and upon every fowl of the air, upon all that moveth upon the earth, and upon all the fishes of the sea; into your hand are they delivered. *Genesis 9:2*

Behold, I give unto you power to tread on serpents and scorpions, and over all the power of the enemy: and nothing shall by any means hurt you.

Luke 10:19

And what is the exceeding greatness of His power to us-ward who believe, according to the working of His mighty power, And hath put all things under His feet, and gave Him to be the head over all things to the church, Which is His body, the fulness of Him that filleth all in all. *Ephesians 1:19, 22-23*

6

Church

I was glad when they said unto me, Let us go into the house of the Lord.   *Psalm 122:1*

No weapon that is formed against thee shall prosper; and every tongue that shall rise against thee in judgment thou shalt condemn. This is the heritage of the servants of the Lord, and their righteousness is of Me, saith the Lord.   *Isaiah 54:17*

The glory of this latter house shall be greater than of the former, saith the Lord of hosts: and in this place will I give peace, saith the Lord of hosts.
          Haggai 2:9

So we, being many, are one body in Christ, and every one members one of another.   *Romans 12:5*

Now therefore ye are no more strangers and foreigners, but fellowcitizens with the saints, and of the household of God; And are built upon the foundation of the apostles and prophets, Jesus Christ Himself being the chief corner stone; In Whom ye also are builded together for an habitation of God through the Spirit.   *Ephesians 2:19-20, 22*

7

CONFIDENCE

But they that wait upon the Lord shall renew their strength; they shall mount up with wings as eagles; they shall run, and not be weary; and they shall walk, and not faint. *Isaiah 40:31*

Not that we are sufficient of ourselves to think any thing as of ourselves; but our sufficiency is of God. *2 Corinthians 3:5*

And God is able to make all grace abound toward you; that ye, always having all sufficiency in all things, may abound to every good work. *2 Corinthians 9:8*

Being confident of this very thing, that He which hath begun a good work in you will perform it until the day of Jesus Christ. *Philippians 1:6*

Notwithstanding ye have well done, that ye did communicate with my affliction. *Philippians 4:14*

Ye are of God, little children, and have overcome them: because greater is He that is in you, than He that is in the world. *1 John 4:4*

For God hath not given us the spirit of fear; but of power, and of love, and of a sound mind. *2 Timothy 1:7*

8

DELIVERANCE

And I am come down to deliver them out of the hand of the Egyptians, and to bring them up out of that land unto a good land and a large, unto a land flowing with milk and honey; unto the place of the Canaanites, and the Hittites, and the Amorites, and the Perizzites, and the Hivites, and the Jebusites.

Exodus 3:8

But the Lord your God ye shall fear; and He shall deliver you out of the hand of all your enemies.

2 Kings 17:39

He brought me forth also into a large place; He delivered me, because He delighted in me.

Psalm 18:19

Thou art my hiding place; Thou shalt preserve me from trouble; Thou shalt compass me about with songs of deliverance.   *Psalm 32:7*

And it shall come to pass in that day, that his burden shall be taken away from off thy shoulder, and his yoke from off thy neck, and the yoke shall be destroyed because of the anointing.   *Isaiah 10:27*

And the Lord shall deliver me from every evil work, and will preserve me unto His heavenly kingdom: to Whom be glory for ever and ever. Amen.

2 Timothy 4:18

9

ETERNAL LIFE

For I know that my Redeemer liveth, and that He shall stand at the latter day upon the earth: Whom I shall see for myself, and mine eyes shall behold, and not another; though my reins be consumed within me. *Job 19:25, 27*

For whosoever will save his life shall lose it: and whosoever will lose his life for My sake shall find it. For the Son of man shall come in the glory of His Father with His angels; and then He shall reward every man according to his works. *Matthew 16:25, 27*

For God so loved the world, that He gave His only begotten Son, that whosoever believeth in Him should not perish, but have everlasting life. *John 3:16*

For the wages of sin is death; but the gift of God is eternal life through Jesus Christ our Lord. *Romans 6:23*

And this is the record, that God hath given to us eternal life, and this life is in His Son. *1 John 5:11*

And there shall be no night there; and they need no candle, neither light of the sun; for the Lord God giveth them light: and they shall reign for ever and ever. *Revelation 22:5*

∾ **10** ∾

ETERNAL HONOR

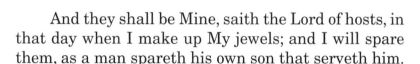

And they shall be Mine, saith the Lord of hosts, in that day when I make up My jewels; and I will spare them, as a man spareth his own son that serveth him.
Malachi 3:17

Blessed is the man that endureth temptation: for when he is tried, he shall receive the crown of life, which the Lord hath promised to them that love Him.
James 1:12

He that hath an ear, let him hear what the Spirit saith unto the churches; To him that overcometh will I give to eat of the hidden manna, and will give him a white stone, and in the stone a new name written, which no man knoweth saving he that receiveth it.
Revelation 2:17

Him that overcometh will I make a pillar in the temple of My God, and he shall go no more out: and I will write upon him the name of My god, and the name of the city of My God, which is new Jerusalem, which cometh down out of heaven from My God: and I will write upon him My new name. To him that overcometh will I grant to sit with Me in My throne, even as I also overcame, and am set down with My Father in His throne. *Revelation 3:12, 21*

11

FAITH

And the Lord said, If ye had faith as a grain of mustard seed, ye might say unto this sycamine tree, Be thou plucked up by the root, and be thou planted in the sea; and it should obey you.   *Luke 17:6*

For therein is the righteousness of God revealed from faith to faith: as it is written, The just shall live by faith.   *Romans 1:17*

Therefore being justified by faith, we have peace with God through our Lord Jesus Christ: By Whom also we have access by faith into this grace wherein we stand, and rejoice in hope of the glory of God.
                    Romans 5:1-2

For I say, through the grace given unto me, to every man that is among you, not to think of himself more highly than he ought to think; but to think soberly, according as God hath dealt to every man the measure of faith.   *Romans 12:3*

But that no man is justified by the law in the sight of God, it is evident: for, The just shall live by faith.   *Galatians 3:11*

Now faith is the substance of things hoped for, the evidence of things not seen.   *Hebrews 11:1*

～ **12** ～

FAITHFULNESS OF GOD

God is not a man, that He should lie; neither the Son of man, that He should repent: hath He said, and shall He not do it? or hath He spoken, and shall He not make it good?   *Numbers 23:19*

Blessed be the Lord, that hath given rest unto His people Israel, according to all that He promised: there hath not failed one word of all His good promise, which He promised by the hand of Moses His servant.
                    1 Kings 8:56

He will not suffer thy foot to be moved: He that keepeth thee will not slumber. Behold, He that keepeth Israel shall neither slumber nor sleep.
                    Psalm 121:3-4

For the mountains shall depart, and the hills be removed; but My kindness shall not depart from thee, neither shall the covenant of My peace be removed, saith the Lord that hath mercy on thee. *Isaiah 54:10*

13

FAMILY

That in blessing I will bless thee, and in multiplying I will multiply thy seed as the stars of the heaven, and as the sand which is upon the sea shore; and thy seed shall possess the gate of his enemies; And in thy seed shall all the nations of the earth be blessed; because thou hast obeyed My voice.
Genesis 22:17-18

And thy seed shall be as the dust of the earth, and thou shalt spread abroad to the west, and to the east, and to the north, and to the south: and in thee and in thy seed shall all the families of the earth be blessed. *Genesis 28:14*

God setteth the solitary in families: He bringeth out those which are bound with chains: but the rebellious dwell in a dry land. *Psalm 68:6*

Lo, children are an heritage of the Lord: and the fruit of the womb is His reward. *Psalm 127:3*

And they said, Believe on the Lord Jesus Christ, and thou shalt be saved, and thy house. *Acts 16:31*

14

FAVOR

And I will make of thee a great nation, and I will bless thee, and make thy name great; and thou shalt be a blessing. *Genesis 12:2*

For Thou, Lord, wilt bless the righteous; with favour wilt Thou compass him as with a shield.
Psalm 5:12

For His anger endureth but a moment; in His favour is life: weeping may endure for a night, but joy cometh in the morning. Lord, by Thy favour Thou hast made my mountain to stand strong: Thou didst hide Thy face, and I was troubled. *Psalm 30:5, 7*

So shalt thou find favour and good understanding in the sight of God and man. *Proverbs 3:4*

For whoso findeth Me findeth life, and shall obtain favour of the Lord. *Proverbs 8:35*

In the light of the king's countenance is life; and his favour is as a cloud of the latter rain.
Proverbs 16:15

❧ 15 ❧

FELLOWSHIP WITH GOD

And the Lord, He it is that doth go before thee; He will be with thee, He will not fail thee, neither forsake thee: fear not, neither be dismayed.

Deuteronomy 31:8

But whoso hearkeneth unto Me shall dwell safely, and shall be quiet from fear of evil. *Proverbs 1:33*

And ye shall seek Me, and find Me, when ye shall search for Me with all your heart. *Jeremiah 29:13*

For whosoever shall do the will of My Father which is in heaven, the same is My brother, and sister, and mother. *Matthew 12:50*

Jesus answered and said unto him, If a man love Me, he will keep My words: and My Father will love him, and We will come unto him, and make Our abode with him. *John 14:23*

Behold, I stand at the door, and knock: if any man hear My voice, and open the door, I will come in to him, and will sup with him, and he with Me.

Revelation 3:20

❧ **16** ❧

FORGIVENESS

If Thou, Lord, shouldest mark iniquities, O Lord, who shall stand? But there is forgiveness with Thee, that Thou mayest be feared.   *Psalm 130:3-4*

I, even I, am He that blotteth out thy transgressions for Mine own sake, and will not remember thy sins.   *Isaiah 43:25*

For if ye forgive men their trespasses, your heavenly Father will also forgive you.   *Matthew 6:14*

And you, being dead in your sins and the uncircumcision of your flesh, hath He quickened together with Him, having forgiven you all trespasses; Blotting out the handwriting of ordinances that was against us, which was contrary to us, and took it out of the way, nailing it to His cross.   *Colossians 2:13-14*

❦ **17** ❦

FREEDOM FROM FEAR

God is our refuge and strength, a very present help in trouble. Therefore will not we fear, though the earth be removed, and though the mountains be carried into the midst of the sea.   *Psalm 46:1-2*

What time I am afraid, I will trust in Thee. In God I will praise His word, in God I have put my trust; I will not fear what flesh can do unto me. When I cry unto Thee, then shall mine enemies turn back: this I know; for God is for me.   *Psalm 56:3-4, 9*

The Lord is on my side; I will not fear: what can man do unto me?   *Psalm 118:6*

But the Lord is faithful, Who shall stablish you, and keep you from evil.   *2 Thessalonians 3:3*

For God hath not given us the spirit of fear; but of power, and of love, and of a sound mind.

2 Timothy 1:7

❧ **18** ❧

FREEDOM FROM WORRY

I laid me down and slept; I awaked; for the Lord sustained me. I will not be afraid of ten thousands of people, that have set themselves against me round about. *Psalm 3:5-6*

Cast thy burden upon the Lord, and He shall sustain thee: He shall never suffer the righteous to be moved. *Psalm 55:22*

When thou passest through the waters, I will be with thee; and through the rivers, they shall not overflow thee: when thou walkest through the fire, thou shalt not be burned; neither shall the flame kindle upon thee. *Isaiah 43:2*

Take therefore no thought for the morrow: for the morrow shall take thought for the things of itself. Sufficient unto the day is the evil thereof. *Matthew 6:34*

But straightway Jesus spake unto them, saying, Be of good cheer; it is I; be not afraid. *Matthew 14:27*

Casting all your care upon Him; for He careth for you. *1 Peter 5:7*

And when I saw Him, I fell at His feet as dead. And He laid His right hand upon me, saying unto me, Fear not; I am the first and the last: I am He that liveth, and was dead; and, behold, I am alive for evermore, Amen; and have the keys of hell and of death. *Revelation 1:17-18*

19

FRIENDSHIP

A friend loveth at all times, and a brother is born for adversity.   *Proverbs 17:17*

A man that hath friends must shew himself friendly: and there is a friend that sticketh closer than a brother.   *Proverbs 18:24*

Thine own friend, and thy father's friend, forsake not; neither go into thy brother's house in the day of thy calamity: for better is a neighbour that is near than a brother far off.   *Proverbs 27:10*

But thou, Israel, art My servant, Jacob whom I have chosen, the seed of Abraham My friend.
                              Isaiah 41:8

Greater love hath no man than this, that a man lay down his life for his friends. Ye are My friends, if ye do whatsoever I command you.   *John 15:13-14*

Henceforth I call you not servants; for the servant knoweth not what his lord doeth: but I have called you friends; for all things that I have heard of My Father I have made known unto you.   *John 15:15*

⟋ **20** ⟍

FRUITFULNESS

Blessed shall be the fruit of thy body, and the fruit of thy ground, and the fruit of thy cattle, the increase of thy kine, and the flocks of thy sheep.

Deuteronomy 28:4

And he shall be like a tree planted by the rivers of water, that bringeth forth his fruit in his season; his leaf also shall not wither; and whatsoever he doeth shall prosper. *Psalm 1:3*

They shall still bring forth fruit in old age; they shall be fat and flourishing. *Psalm 92:14*

For the seed shall be prosperous; the vine shall give her fruit, and the ground shall give her increase, and the heavens shall give their dew; and I will cause the remnant of this people to possess all these things.

Zechariah 8:12

Herein is My Father glorified, that ye bear much fruit; so shall ye be My disciples. *John 15:8*

But the fruit of the Spirit is love, joy, peace, long-suffering, gentleness, goodness, faith, Meekness, temperance: against such there is no law.

Galatians 5:22-23

21

GRACE

As far as the east is from the west, so far hath He removed our transgressions from us. Like as a father pitieth his children, so the Lord pitieth them that fear Him. For He knoweth our frame; He remembereth that we are dust. *Psalm 103:12-14*

But He was wounded for our transgressions, He was bruised for our iniquities: the chastisement of our peace was upon Him; and with His stripes we are healed. *Isaiah 53:5*

Moreover the law entered, that the offence might abound. But where sin abounded, grace did much more abound. *Romans 5:20*

And He said unto me, My grace is sufficient for thee: for My strength is made perfect in weakness. Most gladly therefore will I rather glory in my infirmities, that the power of Christ may rest upon me. *2 Corinthians 12:9*

For by grace are ye saved through faith; and that not of yourselves: it is the gift of God. *Ephesians 2:8*

Let us therefore come boldly unto the throne of grace, that we may obtain mercy, and find grace to help in time of need. *Hebrews 4:16*

⇜ **22** ⇝

GUIDANCE

The meek will He guide in judgment: and the meek will He teach His way.   *Psalm 25:9*

I will instruct thee and teach thee in the way which thou shalt go: I will guide thee with Mine eye.
                                                    Psalm 32:8

Nevertheless I am continually with Thee: Thou hast holden me by my right hand. Thou shalt guide me with Thy counsel, and afterward receive me to glory. Whom have I in heaven but Thee? and there is none upon earth that I desire beside Thee.
                                            Psalm 73:23-25

Even there shall Thy hand lead me, and Thy right hand shall hold me. If I say, Surely the darkness shall cover me; even the night shall be light about me.
                                          Psalm 139:10-11

In all thy ways acknowledge Him, and He shall direct thy paths.   *Proverbs 3:6*

And thine ears shall hear a word behind thee, saying, This is the way, walk ye in it, when ye turn to the right hand, and when ye turn to the left.
                                              Isaiah 30:21

They shall not hunger nor thirst; neither shall the heat nor sun smite them: for He that hath mercy on them shall lead them, even by the springs of water shall He guide them.   *Isaiah 49:10*

23

HAPPINESS

Delight thyself also in the Lord; and He shall give thee the desires of thine heart. Commit thy way unto the Lord; trust also in Him; and He shall bring it to pass.   *Psalm 37:4-5*

Thus will I bless Thee while I live: I will lift up my hands in Thy name. My soul shall be satisfied as with marrow and fatness; and my mouth shall praise Thee with joyful lips.   *Psalm 63:4-5*

The righteous shall be glad in the Lord, and shall trust in Him; and all the upright in heart shall glory.
Psalm 64:10

For the Lord God is a sun and shield: the Lord will give grace and glory: no good thing will He withhold from them that walk uprightly. *Psalm 84:11*

Happy is the man that findeth wisdom, and the man that getteth understanding.   *Proverbs 3:13*

The thief cometh not, but for to steal, and to kill, and to destroy: I am come that they might have life, and that they might have it more abundantly.
John 10:10

If ye know these things, happy are ye if ye do them.   *John 13:17*

~ **24** ~

HEALTH

And said, If thou wilt diligently hearken to the voice of the Lord thy God, and wilt do that which is right in His sight, and wilt give ear to His commandments, and keep all His statutes, I will put none of these diseases upon thee, which I have brought upon the Egyptians: for I am the Lord that healeth thee.
Exodus 15:26

Bless the Lord, O my soul, and forget not all His benefits: Who forgiveth all thine iniquities; Who healeth all thy diseases. *Psalm 103:2-3*

He healeth the broken in heart, and bindeth up their wounds. *Psalm 147:3*

For I will restore health unto thee, and I will heal thee of thy wounds, saith the Lord; because they called thee an Outcast, saying, This is Zion, whom no man seeketh after. *Jeremiah 30:17*

And Jesus went about all the cities and villages, teaching in their synagogues, and preaching the gospel of the kingdom, and healing every sickness and every disease among the people. *Matthew 9:35*

Who His own self bare our sins in His own body on the tree, that we, being dead to sins, should live unto righteousness: by Whose stripes ye were healed.
1 Peter 2:24

25

HEAVEN

And they that be wise shall shine as the brightness of the firmament; and they that turn many to righteousness as the stars for ever and ever.
Daniel 12:3

Verily I say unto you, I will drink no more of the fruit of the vine, until that day that I drink it new in the kingdom of God. *Mark 14:25*

In My Father's house are many mansions: if it were not so, I would have told you. I go to prepare a place for you. *John 14:2*

But as it is written, Eye hath not seen, nor ear heard, neither have entered into the heart of man, the things which God hath prepared for them that love Him. *1 Corinthians 2:9*

For now we see through a glass, darkly; but then face to face: now I know in part; but then shall I know even as also I am known. *1 Corinthians 13:12*

And I heard a great voice out of heaven saying, Behold, the tabernacle of God is with men, and He will dwell with them, and they shall be His people, and God Himself shall be with them, and be their God. And God shall wipe away all tears from their eyes; and there shall be no more death, neither sorrow, nor crying, neither shall there be any more pain: for the former things are passed away. *Revelation 21:3-4*

☙ **26** ☙

HOLY SPIRIT

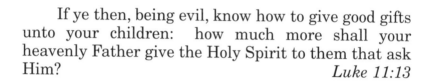

If ye then, being evil, know how to give good gifts unto your children: how much more shall your heavenly Father give the Holy Spirit to them that ask Him?
Luke 11:13

He that believeth on Me, as the scripture hath said, out of his belly shall flow rivers of living water.
John 7:38

But the Comforter, which is the Holy Ghost, Whom the Father will send in My name, He shall teach you all things, and bring all things to your remembrance, whatsoever I have said unto you.
John 14:26

Howbeit when He, the Spirit of truth, is come, He will guide you into all truth: for He shall not speak of Himself; but whatsoever He shall hear, that shall He speak: and He will shew you things to come.
John 16:13

For what man knoweth the things of a man, save the spirit of man which is in him? even so the things of God knoweth no man, but the Spirit of God. Now we have received, not the spirit of the world, but the Spirit which is of God; that we might know the things that are freely given to us of God.
1 Corinthians 2:11-12

27

HOPE

For Thou art my hope, O Lord God: Thou art my trust from my youth.   *Psalm 71:5*

Remember the word unto Thy servant, upon which Thou has caused me to hope. My soul fainteth for Thy salvation: but I hope in Thy word.
Psalm 119:49, 81

And patience, experience; and experience, hope: And hope maketh not ashamed; because the love of God is shed abroad in our hearts by the Holy Ghost which is given unto us.   *Romans 5:4-5*

For we are saved by hope: but hope that is seen is not hope: for what a man seeth, why doth he yet hope for?   *Romans 8:24*

Now the God of hope fill you with all joy and peace in believing, that ye may abound in hope, through the power of the Holy Ghost. *Romans 15:13*

Which hope we have as an anchor of the soul, both sure and stedfast, and which entereth into that within the veil.   *Hebrews 6:19*

❧ 28 ❧

INSPIRATION

———❦◦❦———

But there is a spirit in man: and the inspiration of the Almighty giveth them understanding. *Job 32:8*

Unless Thy law had been my delights, I should then have perished in mine affliction. Thy word is a lamp unto my feet, and a light unto my path.
Psalm 119:92, 105

The spirit of man is the candle of the Lord, searching all the inward parts of the belly.
Proverbs 20:27

For the Holy Ghost shall teach you in the same hour what ye ought to say. *Luke 12:12*

Finally, brethren, whatsoever things are true, whatsoever things are honest, whatsoever things are just, whatsoever things are pure, whatsoever things are lovely, whatsoever things are of good report; if there be any virtue, and if there be any praise, think on these things. *Philippians 4:8*

I can do all things through Christ which strengtheneth me. *Philippians 4:13*

29

INTERCESSION (PRAYER)

Therefore will I divide Him a portion with the great, and He shall divide the spoil with the strong; because He hath poured out His soul unto death: and He was numbered with the transgressors; and He bare the sin of many, and made intercession for the transgressors.   *Isaiah 53:12*

Therefore I say unto you, What things soever ye desire, when ye pray, believe that ye receive them, and ye shall have them.   *Mark 11:24*

And He that searcheth the hearts knoweth what is the mind of the Spirit, because He maketh intercession for the saints according to the will of God.

Romans 8:27

For if I pray in an unknown tongue, my spirit prayeth, but my understanding is unfruitful. What is it then? I will pray with the Spirit, and I will pray with the understanding also: I will sing with the Spirit, and I will sing with the understanding also.

1 Corinthians 14:14-15

⟨ **30** ⟩

JOY

Then he said unto them, Go your way, eat the fat, and drink the sweet, and send portions unto them for whom nothing is prepared: for this day is holy unto our Lord: neither be ye sorry; for the joy of the Lord is your strength. *Nehemiah 8:10*

But Thou, O Lord, art a shield for me; my glory, and the lifter up of mine head. *Psalm 3:3*

Thou wilt shew me the path of life: in Thy presence is fulness of joy; at Thy right hand there are pleasures for evermore. *Psalm 16:11*

For His anger endureth but a moment; in His favour is life: weeping may endure for a night, but joy cometh in the morning. *Psalm 30:5*

This is the day which the Lord hath made; we will rejoice and be glad in it. *Psalm 118:24*

They that sow in tears shall reap in joy. He that goeth forth and weepeth, bearing precious seed, shall doubtless come again with rejoicing, bringing his sheaves with him. *Psalm 126:5-6*

Therefore with joy shall ye draw water out of the wells of salvation. *Isaiah 12:3*

Therefore the redeemed of the Lord shall return, and come with singing unto Zion; and everlasting joy shall be upon their head: they shall obtain gladness and joy; and sorrow and mourning shall flee away. *Isaiah 51:11*

❦ 31 ❦

JUSTICE

————————◆>-o-<◆————————

Doth God pervert judgment? or doth the Almighty pervert justice? *Job 8:3*

Touching the Almighty, we cannot find Him out: He is excellent in power, and in judgment, and in plenty of justice: He will not afflict. *Job 37:23*

He will judge the poor of the people, He shall save the children of the needy, and shall break in pieces the oppressor. *Psalm 72:4*

Justice and judgment are the habitation of Thy throne: mercy and truth shall go before Thy face. *Psalm 89:14*

For the Lord is our judge, the Lord is our lawgiver, the Lord is our king; He will save us. *Isaiah 33:22*

Thus sayeth the Lord, Keep ye judgment, and do justice: for My salvation is near to come, and My righteousness to be revealed. *Isaiah 56:1*

For I know nothing by myself; yet am I not hereby justified: but He that judgeth me is the Lord. *1 Corinthians 4:4*

☞ **32** ☜

KNOWLEDGE

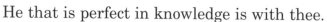

He that is perfect in knowledge is with thee.

Job 36:4

He that chastiseth the heathen, shall not He correct? He that teacheth man knowledge, shall not He know?

Psalm 94:10

I wisdom dwell with prudence, and find out knowledge of witty inventions.

Proverbs 8:12

The fear of the Lord is the beginning of wisdom: and the knowledge of the holy is understanding.

Proverbs 9:10

And wisdom and knowledge shall be the stability of thy times, and strength of salvation: the fear of the Lord is His treasure.

Isaiah 33:6

That ye might walk worthy of the Lord unto all pleasing, being fruitful in every good work, and increasing in the knowledge of God. *Colossians 1:10*

⤳ **33** ⤳

LONGEVITY

Thou shalt keep therefore His statutes, and His commandments, which I command thee this day, that it may go well with thee, and with thy children after thee, and that thou mayest prolong thy days upon the earth, which the Lord thy God giveth thee, forever.

Deuteronomy 4:40

That your days may be multiplied, and the days of your children, in the land which the Lord sware unto your fathers to give them, as the days of heaven upon the earth. *Deuteronomy 11:21*

He asked life of Thee, and Thou gavest it him, even length of days for ever and ever. *Psalm 21:4*

With long life will I satisfy him, and shew him My salvation. *Psalm 91:16*

My son, forget not My law; but let thine heart keep My commandments: For length of days, and long life, and peace, shall they add to thee. *Proverbs 3:1-2*

For by Me thy days shall be multiplied, and the years of thy life shall be increased. *Proverbs 9:11*

≈ **34** ≈

LOVE

For God so loved the world, that He gave His only begotten Son, that whosoever believeth in Him should not perish, but have everlasting life.   *John 3:16*

If ye keep My commandments, ye shall abide in My love; even as I have kept My Father's commandments, and abide in His love. This is My commandment, That ye love one another, as I have loved you.   *John 15:10, 12*

But God commandeth His love toward us, in that, while we were yet sinners, Christ died for us.
      Romans 5:8

For I am persuaded, that neither death, nor life, nor angels, nor principalities, nor powers, nor things present, nor things to come, Nor height, nor depth, nor any other creature, shall be able to separate us from the love of God, which is in Christ Jesus our Lord.
      Romans 8:38-39

He that loveth not knoweth not God; for God is love.   *1 John 4:8*

Herein is love, not that we loved God, but that He loved us, and sent His Son to be the propitiation for our sins.   *1 John 4:10*

35

MARRIAGE

Therefore shall a man leave his father and his mother, and shall cleave unto his wife: and they shall be one flesh.
Genesis 2:24

Thy wife shall be as a fruitful vine by the sides of thine house: thy children like olive plants round about thy table.
Psalm 128:3

Whoso findeth a wife findeth a good thing, and obtaineth favour of the Lord.
Proverbs 18:22

The heart of her husband doth safely trust in her, so that he shall have no need of spoil. She will do him good and not evil all the days of her life.
Proverbs 31:11-12

For the unbelieving husband is sanctified by the wife, and the unbelieving wife is sanctified by the husband: else were your children unclean; but now are they holy.
1 Corinthians 7:14

Husbands, love your wives, even as Christ also loved the church, and gave Himself for it; So ought men to love their wives as their own bodies. He that loveth his wife loveth himself. For this cause shall a man leave his father and mother, and shall be joined unto his wife, and they two shall be one flesh.
Ephesians 5:25, 28, 31

≈ **36** ≈

MERCY

And the bow shall be in the cloud; and I will look upon it, that I may remember the everlasting covenant between God and every living creature of all flesh that is upon the earth.   *Genesis 9:16*

But the Lord was with Joseph, and shewed him mercy, and gave him favour in the sight of the keeper of the prison.   *Genesis 39:21*

And He said, I will make all My goodness pass before thee, and I will proclaim the name of the Lord before thee; and will be gracious to whom I will be gracious, and will shew mercy on whom I will shew mercy.   *Exodus 33:19*

(For the Lord thy God is a merciful God;) He will not forsake thee, neither destroy thee, nor forget the covenant of thy fathers which He sware unto them.
Deuteronomy 4:31

Thy mercy, O Lord, is in the heavens; and Thy faithfulness reacheth unto the clouds.   *Psalm 36:5*

For Thou, Lord, art good, and ready to forgive; and plenteous in mercy unto all them that call upon Thee. In the day of my trouble I will call upon Thee: for Thou wilt answer me.   *Psalm 86:5, 7*

The Lord is gracious, and full of compassion; slow to anger, and of great mercy. The Lord is good to all: and His tender mercies are over all His works.
Psalm 145:8-9

✺ 37 ✺

MIRACLES

And Moses stretched forth his hand over the sea, and the sea returned to his strength when the morning appeared; and the Egyptians fled against it; and the Lord overthrew the Egyptians in the midst of the sea. And the waters returned, and covered the chariots, and the horsemen, and all the host of Pharaoh that came into the sea after them; there remained not so much as one of them. But the children of Israel walked upon dry land in the midst of the sea; and the waters were a wall unto them on their right hand, and on their left. *Exodus 14:27-29*

He spread a cloud for a covering; and fire to give light in the night. The people asked, and He brought quails, and satisfied them with the bread of heaven.
Psalm 105:39-40

But Jesus beheld them, and said unto them, With men this is impossible; but with God all things are possible. *Matthew 19:26*

For verily I say unto you, That whosoever shall say unto this mountain, Be thou removed, and be thou cast into the sea; and shall not doubt in his heart, but shall believe that those things which he saith shall come to pass; he shall have whatsoever he saith. Therefore I say unto you, What things soever ye desire, when ye pray, believe that ye receive them, and ye shall have them. *Mark 11:23-24*

❧ **38** ❧

MINISTRY

The Spirit of the Lord God is upon me; because the Lord hath anointed me to preach good tidings unto the meek; He hath sent me to bind up the broken-hearted, to proclaim liberty to the captives, and the opening of the prison to them that are bound.

Isaiah 61:1

For many are called, but few are chosen.

Matthew 22:14

Ye have not chosen Me, but I have chosen you, and ordained you, that ye should go and bring forth fruit, and that your fruit should remain: that whatsoever ye shall ask of the Father in My name, He may give it you. *John 15:16*

And how shall they preach, except they be sent? as it is written, How beautiful are the feet of them that preach the gospel of peace, and bring glad tidings of good things! *Romans 10:15*

And He gave some, apostles; and some, prophets; and some, evangelists; and some, pastors and teachers. *Ephesians 4:11*

39

PEACE

And I will give peace in the land, and ye shall lie down, and none shall make you afraid: and I will rid evil beasts out of the land, neither shall the sword go through your land. *Leviticus 26:6*

The Lord will give strength unto His people; the Lord will bless His people with peace. *Psalm 29:11*

In His days shall the righteous flourish; and abundance of peace so long as the moon endureth. *Psalm 72:7*

Thou wilt keep him in perfect peace, whose mind is stayed on Thee: because he trusteth in Thee. *Isaiah 26:3*

And all thy children shall be taught of the Lord; and great shall be the peace of thy children. *Isaiah 54:13*

And the peace of God, which passeth all understanding, shall keep your hearts and minds through Christ Jesus. *Philippians 4:7*

Now the Lord of peace Himself give you peace always by all means. The Lord be with you all. *2 Thessalonians 3:16*

And the fruit of righteousness is sown in peace of them that make peace. *James 3:18*

≈ **40** ≈

POWER

And in very deed for this cause have I raised thee up, for to shew in thee My power; and that My name may be declared throughout all the earth.

Exodus 9:16

And because He loved thy fathers, therefore He chose their seed after them, and brought thee out in His sight with His mighty power out of Egypt.

Deuteronomy 4:37

There shall no man be able to stand before you: for the Lord your God shall lay the fear of you and the dread of you upon all the land that ye shall tread upon, as He hath said unto you.   *Deuteronomy 11:25*

When the enemy shall come in like a flood, the Spirit of the Lord shall lift up a standard against him.

Isaiah 59:19

And when He had called unto Him His twelve disciples, He gave them power against unclean spirits, to cast them out, and to heal all manner of sickness and all manner of disease. Heal the sick, cleanse the lepers, raise the dead, cast out devils: freely ye have received, freely give.   *Matthew 10:1, 8*

Verily, verily, I say unto you, He that believeth on Me, the works that I do shall he do also; and greater works than these shall he do; because I go unto My Father.   *John 14:12*

41

PROMOTION

And the Lord shall make thee the head, and not the tail; and thou shalt be above only, and thou shalt not be beneath; if that thou hearken unto the commandments of the Lord thy God, which I command thee this day, to observe and to do them.

Deuteronomy 28:13

He raiseth up the poor out of the dust, and lifteth up the beggar from the dunghill, to set them among princes, and to make them inherit the throne of glory: for the pillars of the earth are the Lord's, and He hath set the world upon them.

1 Samuel 2:8

Thou shalt increase my greatness, and comfort me on every side.

Psalm 71:21

Blessed are the meek: for they shall inherit the earth.

Matthew 5:5

But woe unto you, scribes and Pharisees, hypocrites! for ye shut up the kingdom of heaven against men: for ye neither go in yourselves, neither suffer ye them that are entering to go in.

Matthew 23:13

And hath raised us up together, and made us sit together in heavenly places in Christ Jesus.

Ephesians 2:6

Humble yourselves therefore under the mighty hand of God, that He may exalt you in due time.

1 Peter 5:6

42

PROSPERITY

And the Lord said unto Abram, after that Lot was separated from him, Lift up now thine eyes, and look from the place where thou art northward, and southward, and eastward, and westward: For all the land which thou seest, to thee will I give it, and to thy seed for ever.
Genesis 13:14-15

But I have said unto you, Ye shall inherit their land, and I will give it unto you to possess it, a land that floweth with milk and honey: I am the Lord your God, which have separated you from other people.
Leviticus 20:24

For I will have respect unto you, and make you fruitful, and multiply you, and establish My covenant with you.
Leviticus 26:9

And he sought God in the days of Zechariah, who had understanding in the visions of God: and as long as he sought the Lord, God made him to prosper.
2 Chronicles 26:5

Beloved, I wish above all things that thou mayest prosper and be in health, even as thy soul prospereth.
3 John 1:2

43

PROTECTION

The Lord your God which goeth before you, He shall fight for you, according to all that He did for you in Egypt before your eyes.   *Deuteronomy 1:30*

Be not afraid nor dismayed by reason of this great multitude; for the battle is not yours, but God's.
                    2 Chronicles 20:15

I will say of the Lord, He is my refuge and my fortress: my God; in Him will I trust. Surely He shall deliver thee from the snare of the fowler, and from the noisome pestilence. He shall cover thee with His feathers, and under His wings shalt thou trust: His truth shall be thy shield and buckler. Thou shalt not be afraid for the terror by night; nor for the arrow that flieth by day; Nor for the pestilence that walketh in darkness; nor for the destruction that wasteth at noonday.   *Psalm 91:2-6*

When thou passest through the waters, I will be with thee: and through the rivers, they shall not overflow thee: when thou walkest through the fire, thou shalt not be burned; neither shall the flame kindle upon thee.   *Isaiah 43:2*

The Lord is good, a strong hold in the day of trouble; and He knoweth them that trust in Him.
                    Nahum 1:7

But even the very hairs of your head are all numbered. Fear not therefore: ye are of more value than many sparrows.   *Luke 12:7*

❦ 44 ❦

PROVISION

For the Lord thy God bringeth thee into a good land, a land of brooks of water, of fountains and depths that spring out of valleys and hills; A land of wheat, and barley, and vines, and fig trees, and pomegranates; a land of oil olive, and honey; A land wherein thou shalt eat bread without scarceness, thou shalt not lack any thing in it; a land whose stones are iron, and out of whose hills thou mayest dig brass.

Deuteronomy 8:7-9

Blessed shalt thou be in the city, and blessed shalt thou be in the field. Blessed shall be the fruit of thy body, and the fruit of thy ground, and the fruit of thy cattle, the increase of thy kine, and the flocks of thy sheep. *Deuteronomy 28:3-4*

For thus saith the Lord God of Israel, The barrel of meal shall not waste, neither shall the cruse of oil fail, until the day that the Lord sendeth rain upon the earth. *1 Kings 17:14*

Trust in the Lord, and do good; so shalt thou dwell in the land, and verily thou shalt be fed. I have been young, and now am old; yet have I not seen the righteous forsaken, nor His seed begging bread.

Psalm 37:3, 25

Blessed be the Lord, Who daily loadeth us with benefits, even the God of our salvation. *Psalm 68:19*

The eyes of all wait upon Thee; and Thou givest them their meat in due season. *Psalm 145:15*

45

REST

I will both lay me down in peace, and sleep: for Thou, Lord, only makest me dwell in safety.
Psalm 4:8

He maketh me to lie down in green pastures: He leadeth me beside the still waters. *Psalm 23:2*

But whoso hearkeneth unto Me shall dwell safely, and shall be quiet from fear of evil. *Proverbs 1:33*

When thou liest down, thou shalt not be afraid: yea, thou shalt lie down, and thy sleep shall be sweet.
Proverbs 3:24

And it shall come to pass in the day that the Lord shall give thee rest from thy sorrow, and from thy fear, and from the hard bondage wherein thou wast made to serve. *Isaiah 14:3*

Come unto Me, all ye that labour and are heavy laden, and I will give you rest. *Matthew 11:28*

46

RESTORATION

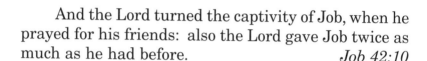

And the Lord turned the captivity of Job, when he prayed for his friends: also the Lord gave Job twice as much as he had before.   *Job 42:10*

He restoreth my soul: He leadeth me in the paths of righteousness for His name's sake.   *Psalm 23:3*

He brought me up also out of an horrible pit, out of the miry clay, and set my feet upon a rock, and established my goings. And He hath put a new song in my mouth, even praise unto our God: many shall see it, and fear, and shall trust in the Lord.
                                             Psalm 40:2-3

Who satisfieth thy mouth with good things; so that thy youth is renewed like the eagle's.
                                             Psalm 103:5

In the day when I cried Thou answeredst me, and strengthenedst me with strength in my soul. Though I walk in the midst of trouble, Thou wilt revive me.
                                             Psalm 138:3, 7

Therefore if any man be in Christ, he is a new creature: old things are passed away; behold, all things are become new.   *2 Corinthians 5:17*

47

RESURRECTION

He will swallow up death in victory; and the Lord God will wipe away tears from off all faces; and the rebuke of His people shall He take away from off all the earth: for the Lord hath spoken it.   *Isaiah 25:8*

For as the Father raiseth up the dead, and quickeneth them; even so the Son quickeneth whom He will.   *John 5:21*

Jesus said unto her, I am the resurrection, and the life: he that believeth in Me, though he were dead, yet shall he live: And whosoever liveth and believeth in Me shall never die. Believest thou this?
     John 11:25-26

For if we have been planted together in the likeness of His death, we shall be also in the likeness of His resurrection.   *Romans 6:5*

But if the Spirit of Him that raised up Jesus from the dead dwell in you, He that raised up Christ from the dead shall also quicken your mortal bodies by His Spirit that dwelleth in you.   *Romans 8:11*

48

RICHES

But thou shalt remember the Lord thy God: for it is He that giveth thee power to get wealth, that He may establish His covenant which He sware unto thy fathers, as it is this day.   *Deuteronomy 8:18*

Both riches and honour come of Thee, and Thou reignest over all; and in Thine hand is power and might; and in Thine hand it is to make great, and to give strength unto all.   *1 Chronicles 29:12*

Riches and honour are with Me; yea, durable riches and righteousness. My fruit is better than gold, yea, than fine gold; and My revenue than choice silver.   *Proverbs 8:18-19*

By humility and the fear of the Lord are riches, and honour, and life.   *Proverbs 22:4*

Every man also to whom God hath given riches and wealth, and hath given him power to eat thereof, and to take his portion, and to rejoice in his labour; this is the gift of God.   *Ecclesiastes 5:19*

And I will give thee the treasures of darkness, and hidden riches of secret places, that thou mayest know that I, the Lord, which call thee by thy name, am the God of Israel.   *Isaiah 45:3*

For ye know the grace of our Lord Jesus Christ, that, though He was rich, yet for your sakes He became poor, that ye through His poverty might be rich.   *2 Corinthians 8:9*

≈ 49 ≈

Salvation

The Lord is my light and my salvation; whom shall I fear? the Lord is the strength of my life; of whom shall I be afraid? *Psalm 27:1*

As for me, I will call upon God; and the Lord shall save me. *Psalm 55:16*

Whoso eateth My flesh, and drinketh My blood, hath eternal life; and I will raise him up at the last day. *John 6:54*

For I am not ashamed of the gospel of Christ: for it is the power of God unto salvation to every one that believeth; to the Jew first, and also to the Greek. *Romans 1:16*

For scarcely for a righteous man will one die: yet peradventure for a good man some would even dare to die. But God commendeth His love toward us, in that, while we were yet sinners, Christ died for us. *Romans 5:7-8*

In Whom we have redemption through His blood, even the forgiveness of sins. *Colossians 1:14*

↝ **50** ↝

SECURITY

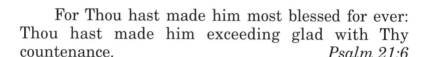

For Thou hast made him most blessed for ever: Thou hast made him exceeding glad with Thy countenance.   *Psalm 21:6*

He shall send from heaven, and save me from the reproach of him that would swallow me up. God shall send forth His mercy and His truth.   *Psalm 57:3*

He only is my rock and my salvation; He is my defence; I shall not be greatly moved. In God is my salvation and my glory: the rock of my strength, and my refuge, is in God.   *Psalm 62:2, 7*

He suffered no man to do them wrong: yea, He reproved kings for their sakes; Saying, Touch not Mine anointed, and do My prophets no harm.
                              Psalm 105:14-15

For he shall be as a tree planted by the waters, and that spreadeth out her roots by the river, and shall not see when heat cometh, but her leaf shall be green; and shall not be careful in the year of drought, neither shall cease from yielding fruit. *Jeremiah 17:8*

And the rain descended, and the floods came, and the winds blew, and beat upon that house; and it fell not: for it was founded upon a rock.   *Matthew 7:25*

⧉ **51** ⧉

STRENGTH

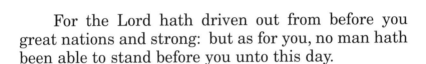

For the Lord hath driven out from before you great nations and strong: but as for you, no man hath been able to stand before you unto this day.
Joshua 23:9

Glory and honour are in His presence; strength and gladness are in His place.   *1 Chronicles 16:27*

The Lord is my rock, and my fortress, and my deliverer; my God, my strength, in Whom I will trust; my buckler, and the horn of my salvation, and my high tower. For by Thee I have run through a troop; and by my God have I leaped over a wall. It is God that girdeth me with strength, and maketh my way perfect.   *Psalm 18:2, 29, 32*

They that trust in the Lord shall be as mount Zion, which cannot be removed, but abideth for ever.
Psalm 125:1

In the day when I cried Thou answeredst me, and strengthenedst me with strength in my soul.
Psalm 138:3

He giveth power to the faint; and to them that have no might He increaseth strength.   *Isaiah 40:29*

But they that wait upon the Lord shall renew their strength; they shall mount up with wings as eagles; they shall run, and not be weary; and they shall walk, and not faint.   *Isaiah 40:31*

❧ **52** ❧

SUCCESS

━━━➢-◦-ⅇ━━━

There shalt not any man be able to stand before thee all the days of thy life: as I was with Moses, so I will be with thee: I will not fail thee, nor forsake thee. Only be thou strong and very courageous, that thou mayest observe to do according to all the law, which Moses My servant commanded thee: turn not from it to the right hand or to the left, that thou mayest prosper withersoever thou goest. This book of the law shall not depart out of thy mouth; but thou shalt meditate therein day and night, that thou mayest observe to do according to all that is written therein: for then thou shalt make thy way prosperous, and then thou shalt have good success. *Joshua 1:5, 7-8*

Praise ye the Lord. Blessed is the man that feareth the Lord, that delighteth greatly in His commandments. His seed shall be mighty upon earth: the generation of the upright shall be blessed. Wealth and riches shall be in His house: and His righteousness endureth for ever. *Psalm 112:1-3*

And the Lord shall guide thee continually, and satisfy thy soul in drought, and make fat thy bones: and thou shalt be like a watered garden, and like a spring of water, whose waters fail not. *Isaiah 58:11*

But seek ye first the kingdom of God, and His righteousness; and all these things shall be added unto you. *Matthew 6:33*

But my God shall supply all your need according to His riches in glory by Christ Jesus. *Philippians 4:19*

～ **53** ～

TRUTH

God is not a man, that He should lie; neither the son of man, that He should repent: hath He said, and shall He not do it? or hath He spoken, and shall He not make it good?   *Numbers 23:19*

His truth shall be thy shield and buckler.
Psalm 91:4

For there is nothing hid, which shall not be manifested; neither was any thing kept secret, but that it should come abroad.   *Mark 4:22*

And ye shall know the truth, and the truth shall make you free.   *John 8:32*

Jesus saith unto him, I am the way, the truth, and the life: no man cometh unto the Father, but by Me.
John 14:6

And for their sakes I sanctify Myself, that they also might be sanctified through the truth.
John 17:19

For the truth's sake, which dwelleth in us, and shall be with us for ever.   *2 John 1:2*

～ **54** ～

UNDERSTANDING

Behold, I have done according to thy words: lo, I have given thee a wise and an understanding heart; so that there was none like thee before thee, neither after thee shall any arise like unto thee.　*1 Kings 3:12*

The fear of the Lord is the beginning of wisdom: a good understanding have all they that do His commandments: His praise endureth for ever.
Psalm 111:10

The entrance of Thy words giveth light; it giveth understanding unto the simple.　*Psalm 119:130*

Discretion shall preserve thee, understanding shall keep thee.　*Proverbs 2:11*

Then opened He their understanding, that they might understand the scriptures.　*Luke 24:45*

The eyes of your understanding being enlightened; that ye may know what is the hope of His calling, and what the riches of the glory of His inheritance in the saints.　*Ephesians 1:18*

Consider what I say; and the Lord give thee understanding in all things.　*2 Timothy 2:7*

❧ 55 ❧

VICTORY

———————◦———————

Through God we shall do valiantly: for He it is that shall tread down our enemies.   *Psalm 60:12*

Through God we shall do valiantly: for He it is that shall tread down our enemies.   *Psalm 108:13*

O death, where is thy sting? O grave, where is thy victory? The sting of death is sin; and the strength of sin is the law. But thanks be to God, which giveth us the victory through our Lord Jesus Christ.
1 Corinthians 15:55-57

Wherefore take unto you the whole armour of God, that ye may be able to withstand in the evil day, and having done all, to stand. Stand therefore, having your loins girt about with truth, and having on the breastplate of righteousness; And your feet shod with the preparation of the gospel of peace; Above all, taking the shield of faith, wherewith ye shall be able to quench all the fiery darts of the wicked. And take the helmet of salvation, and the sword of the Spirit, which is the word of God.   *Ephesians 6:13-17*

For whatsoever is born of God overcometh the world: and this is the victory that overcometh the world, even our faith.   *1 John 5:4*

❧ **56** ❧

WISDOM

And God gave Solomon wisdom and understanding exceeding much, and largeness of heart, even as the sand that is on the sea shore.   *1 Kings 4:29*

For the Lord giveth wisdom: out of His mouth cometh knowledge and understanding. He layeth up sound wisdom for the righteous: He is a buckler to them that walk uprightly.   *Proverbs 2:6-7*

For I will give you a mouth and wisdom, which all your adversaries shall not be able to gainsay nor resist.   *Luke 21:15*

But of Him are ye in Christ Jesus, Who of God is made unto us wisdom, and righteousness, and sanctification, and redemption.   *1 Corinthians 1:30*

Wherein He hath abounded toward us in all wisdom and prudence; That the God of our Lord Jesus Christ, the Father of glory, may give unto you the spirit of wisdom and revelation in the knowledge of Him.   *Ephesians 1:8, 17*

If any of you lack wisdom, let him ask of God, that giveth to all men liberally, and upbraideth not; and it shall be given him.   *James 1:5*

✐ 57 ✐

WORD OF GOD

The law of the Lord is perfect, converting the soul: the testimony of the Lord is sure, making wise the simple. The statutes of the Lord are right, rejoicing the heart: the commandment of the Lord is pure, enlightening the eyes. *Psalm 19:7-8*

He sent His word, and healed them, and delivered them from their destructions. *Psalm 107:20*

Blessed are the undefiled in the way, who walk in the law of the Lord. Blessed are they that keep His testimonies, and that seek Him with the whole heart. Wherewithal shall a young man cleanse his way? by taking heed thereto according to Thy word. And I will walk at liberty: for I seek Thy precepts. This is my comfort in my affliction: for Thy word hath quickened me. *Psalm 119:1-2 ,9, 45, 50*

So shall My word be that goeth forth out of My mouth: it shall not return unto Me void, but it shall accomplish that which I please, and it shall prosper in the thing whereto I sent it. *Isaiah 55:11*

Thy words were found, and I did eat them; and Thy word was unto me the joy and rejoicing of mine heart: for I am called by Thy name, O Lord God of hosts. *Jeremiah 15:16*

58

WORK

Six days thou shalt do thy work, and on the seventh day thou shalt rest.   *Exodus 23:12*

Because that for this thing the Lord thy God shall bless thee in all thy works, and in all that thou puttest thine hand unto.   *Deuteronomy 15:10*

And all these blessings shall come on thee, and overtake thee, if thou shalt hearken unto the voice of the Lord thy God. The Lord shall open unto thee His good treasure, the heaven to give the rain unto thy land in His season, and to bless all the work of thine hand: and thou shalt lend unto many nations, and thou shalt not borrow.   *Deuteronomy 28:2, 12*

And he shall be like a tree planted by the rivers of water, that bringeth forth his fruit in his season; his leaf also shall not wither; and whatsoever he doeth shall prosper.   *Psalm 1:3*

And let the beauty of the Lord our God be upon us: and establish Thou the work of our hands upon us; yea, the work of our hands establish Thou it.
Psalm 90:17

And also that every man should eat and drink, and enjoy the good of all his labour, it is the gift of God.
Ecclesiastes 3:13

DECISION

Will You Accept Jesus As Your Personal Savior Today?

The Bible says, "That if thou shalt confess with thy mouth the Lord Jesus, and shalt believe in thine heart that God hath raised Him from the dead, thou shalt be saved," (Romans 10:9).

Pray this prayer from your heart today!

"Dear Jesus, I believe that You died for me and rose again on the third day. I confess I am a sinner...I need Your love and forgiveness...Come into my heart. Forgive my sins. I receive Your eternal life. Confirm Your love by giving me peace, joy and supernatural love for others. Amen."

☐ Yes, Mike! I made a decision to accept Christ as my personal Savior today. Please send me my free gift of your book, *31 Keys to a New Beginning* to help me with my new life in Christ.

NAME _____ BIRTHDAY _____

ADDRESS _____

CITY _____ STATE ____ ZIP ____

PHONE _____ E-MAIL _____

Mail to: **The Wisdom Center** · 4051 Denton Hwy. · Ft. Worth, TX 76117
1-817-759-BOOK · 1-817-759-0300

You Will Love Our Website...! www.TheWisdomCenter.tv

□ *Yes Mike, I want to join The Wisdom Key 3000.*
  Please rush The Wisdom Key Partnership Pak to me today!
□ *Enclosed is my first monthly Seed-Faith Promise of:*
  □ *$58* □ *Other $_____.*

ECK □MONEY ORDER □AMEX □DISCOVER □MASTERCARD □VISA

Card # _____ Exp. ____/____

ture _____

_____ Birth Date ____/____/____

ss _____

_____ State _____ Zip _____

_____ E-Mail _____

THE WISDOM CENTER 1-817-759-**BOOK**
4051 Denton Highway • Fort Worth, TX 76117   1-817-759-**0300**

— *You Will Love Our Website:* —
www.TheWisdomCenter.tv

It Could Happen To You!

Tax Reduction...!

Since God has brought you into my life with a $58 Seed, it ha[s] turned my life around. God has changed my heart so much because o[f] your Wisdom and your ministry, I never knew God so personally as I a[m] now learning about. I never knew how close to Him I could get and ho[w] much He could change things in my life and in me and in other people['s] lives just by believing that He could. I never knew what taking a step o[f] faith could actually be and what it could do. I'm learning so muc[h] about the Lord that I never knew before.

He also took our back taxes from $75,000 to $5,729 from ou[r] $58 Seed.

J. & A. M. - TN

$58 Seed Of Faith Brings Forth Long Awaite[d] Promotion...!

After planting my first $58 Seed, I received a job promotio[n] that I had prayed about for a year, exults a partner from Sout[h] Carolina. It is a $1,500 a year raise and it's three grades highe[r] than my past position!

C.C. - SC

Partner Gets Results From Talk With God...!

"Lord, I want to help Mike and be a part of this Blessin[g] Covenant, but You will have to give me the $58 because I don['t] have it," confided a partner from Nevada. My blessings starte[d] to arrive even before I sent the money. I received money for m[y] rent and car insurance—God is starting to open the windows o[f] Heaven for me!

R.S. - NV

Millionaire-Talk

31 Things You Will Need To Become A Millionaire
Man-Talk 20

DR. MIKE MURDOCK

31 Things You Will Need To Become A Millionaire (CD/MT-20)

Topics Include:

▶ *You Will Need Financial Heroes*
▶ *Your Willingness To Negotiate Everything*
▶ *You Must Have The Ability To Transfer Your Enthusiasm, Your Vision To Others*
▶ *Know Your Competition*
▶ *Be Willing To Train Your Team Personally As To Your Expectations*
▶ *Hire Professionals To Do A Professional's Job*

I have asked the Lord for 3,000 special partners who will sow an extra Seed of $58 towards the Ministry Outreaches. Your Seed is so appreciated! Remember to request my Gift CD, *31 Things You Will Need To Become A Millionaire,* when you write this week!

THE WISDOM CENTER
4051 Denton Highway • Fort Worth, TX 76117

1-817-759-BOOK
1-817-759-0300

You Will Love Our Website...!
TheWisdomCenter.tv   A

Miracle 7

BOOK PAK!

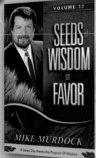

DR. MIKE MURDOCK

❶ Dream Seeds/<u>Book</u> (106pg/B-11/$9)

❷ Seeds of Wisdom on Favor/<u>Book</u> (32pg/B-119/$5)

❸ Seeds of Wisdom on Miracles/<u>Book</u> (32pg/B-15/$3)

❹ Seeds of Wisdom on Prayer/<u>Book</u> (32pg/B-23/$3)

❺ The Jesus Book/<u>Book</u> (166pg/B-27/$10)

❻ The Memory Bible on Miracles/<u>Book</u> (32pg/B-208/$3)

❼ The Mentor's Manna on Attitude/<u>Book</u> (32pg/B-58/$3)

The Wisdom Center
Miracle 7 Book Pak!
Only $**30** $36 Value
WBL-24
Wisdom Is The Principal Thing

Add 10% For S/H

Quantity Prices Available Upon Request

**Each Wisdom Book may be purchased separately if so desired.

  THE WISDOM CENTER
4051 Denton Highway • Fort Worth, TX 76117

1-817-759-BOOK
1-817-759-0300

You Will Love Our Website...!
TheWisdomCenter.tv

Money 7 BOOK PAK!

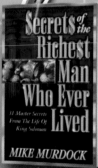
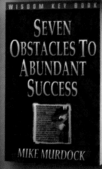
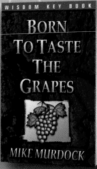

DR. MIKE MURDOCK

❶ Secrets of the Richest Man Who Ever Lived/<u>Book</u> (179pg/B-99/$10)

❷ The Blessing Bible/<u>Book</u> (252pg/B-28/$10)

❸ Born To Taste The Grapes/<u>Book</u> (32pg/B-65/$3)

❹ Creating Tomorrow Through Seed-Faith/<u>Book</u> (32pg/B-06/$5)

❺ Seeds of Wisdom on Prosperity/<u>Book</u> (32pg/B-22/$3)

❻ Seven Obstacles To Abundant Success/<u>Book</u> (32pg/B-64/$3)

❼ Ten Lies Many People Believe About Money/<u>Book</u> (32pg/B-04/$5)

The Wisdom Center
Money 7 Book Pak!
Only $**30** $39 Value
WBL-30
Wisdom Is The Principal Thing

Add 10% For S/H

**Each Wisdom Book may be purchased separately if so desired.

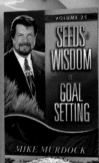

101 Wisdom Keys That Have Most Changed My Life.

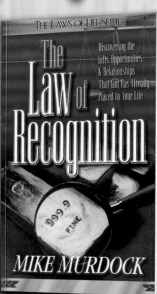

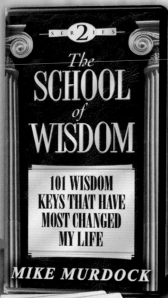

School of Wisdom #2 Pak!

- ▶ What Attracts Others Toward You
- ▶ The Secret Of Multiplying Your Financial Blessings
- ▶ What Stops The Flow Of Your Faith
- ▶ Why Some Fail And Others Succeed
- ▶ How To Discern Your Life Assignment
- ▶ How To Create Currents Of Favor With Others
- ▶ How To Defeat Loneliness
- ▶ 47 Keys In Recognizing The Mate God Has Approved For You
- ▶ 14 Facts You Should Know About Your Gifts And Talents
- ▶ 17 Important Facts You Should Remember About Your Weakness
- ▶ And Much, Much More...

The Wisdom Center
School of Wisdom #2 Pak!
Only $**30**
$40 Value
PAK002
Wisdom Is The Principal Thing

Add 10% For S/H

TS-42

The Businessman's Devotional Book Pak!

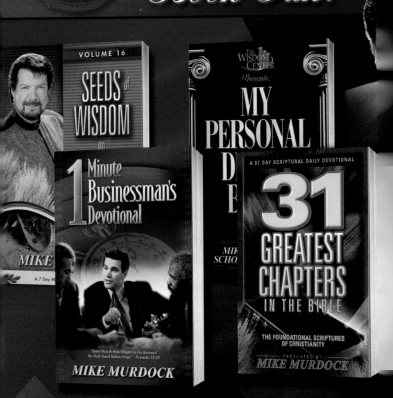

1. **Seeds of Wisdom on Problem-Solving**/<u>Book</u> (32pg/B-

2. **My Personal Dream Book**/<u>Book</u> (32pg/B-143/$5)

3. **1 Minute Businessman's Devotional**
   /<u>Book</u> (224pg/B-42/$12)

4. **31 Greatest Chapters In The Bible**
   /<u>Book</u> (138pg/B-54/$10)

The Wisdo
Th
Businessm
tional 4 B
Only $2
Wisdom Is The
PAK

ach Wisdom Book may be purchased separately if so desired.

Add 10%

The CRISIS COLLECTION

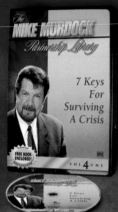

You Get All 6 For One Great Price!

The Wisdom Center
Celebrating 40 Years of Global Ministry!
Wisdom Is The Principal Thing

The Wisdom Center
The Crisis Collection
Only $**40** $57 Value
PAK-16
Wisdom Is The Principal Thing

❶ 7 Keys For Surviving A Crisis/<u>DVD</u> (MMPL-04D/$10)
❷ You Can Make It!/<u>Music</u> CD (MMML-05/$10)
❸ Wisdom For Crisis Times/<u>6 Cassettes</u> (TS-40/$30)
❹ Seeds of Wisdom on Overcoming/<u>Book</u> (32pg/B-17/$3)
❺ Seeds of Wisdom on Motivating Yourself/<u>Book</u> (32pg/B-171/$5)
❻ Wisdom For Crisis Times/<u>Book</u> (112pg/B-40/$9)

Also Included... Two Free Bonus Books!

*Each Wisdom Product may be purchased separately if so desired.

Add 10% For S/H

H **THE WISDOM CENTER** 4051 Denton Highway • Fort Worth, TX 76117
1-817-759-BOOK
1-817-759-0300

— You Will Love Our Website...! —
TheWisdomCenter.tv

THE TURNAROUND Collection

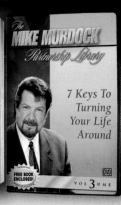
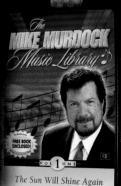

❶ The Wisdom Commentary Vol. 1/<u>Book</u> (256pg/52 Topics/B-136/$20)

❷ Battle Techniques For War-Weary Saints/<u>Book</u> (32pg/B-07/$5)

❸ Seeds of Wisdom on Overcoming/<u>Book</u> (32pg/B-17/$3)

❹ The Memory Bible on Healing/<u>Book</u> (32pg/B-196/$3)

❺ How To Turn Your Mistakes Into Miracles/<u>Book</u> (32pg/B-56/$5)

❻ 7 Keys To Turning Your Life Around/<u>DVD</u> (MMPL-03D/$10)

❼ The Sun Will Shine Again/<u>Music CD</u> (MMML-01/$10)

**Each Wisdom Product may be purchased separately if so desired.

THE WISDOM CENTER
4051 Denton Highway • Fort Worth, TX 76117
1-817-759-BOOK
1-817-759-0300

You Will Love Our Website...!
TheWisdomCenter.tv

Favor 4!

This Collection Of Wisdom Will Change The Seasons Of Your Life Forever!

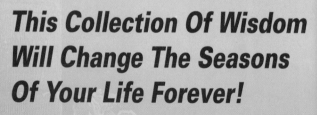

1 The School of Wisdom #4 / 31 Keys To Unleashing Uncommon Favor...Tape Series/<u>6 Cassettes</u> (TS-44/$30)

2 The Hidden Power Of Right Words... The Wisdom Center Pastoral Library/<u>CD</u> (WCPL-27/$10)

3 Seeds of Wisdom on Favor/<u>Book</u> (32pg/B-119/$5)

4 Seeds of Wisdom on Obedience/<u>Book</u> (32pg/B-20/$3)

**Each Wisdom Product may be purchased separately if so desired.

 THE WISDOM CENTER 4051 Denton Highway • Fort Worth, TX 76117

1-817-759-BOOK
1-817-759-0300

—You Will Love Our Website...!—
TheWisdomCenter.tv

J

Financial $ecrets.

THE 31 DAY MENTORSHIP PROGRAM

31 REASON$
PEOPLE DO NOT RECEIVE THEIR
FINANCIAL HARVE$T

MIKE MURDOCK

VIDEO

7 KEYS to 1000 TIMES MORE

*The Lord God Of Your Fathers
Make You A Thousand Times
So Many More As You Are,
And Bless You, As He Hath
Promised You!*
Deuteronomy 1:11

MIKE MURDOCK

VI-16

Your Financial World Will Change Forever.

Video 2-Pak!

8 Scriptural Reasons You Should Pursue Financial Prosperity

The Secret Prayer Key You Need When Making A Financial Request To God

The Weapon Of Expectation And The 5 Miracles It Unlocks

How To Discern Those Who Qualify To Receive Your Financial Assistance

How To Predict The Miracle Moment God Will Schedule Your Financial Breakthrough

Habits Of Uncommon Achievers

The Greatest Success Law I Ever Discovered

How To Discern Your Place Of Assignment, The Only Place Financial Provision Is Guaranteed

3 Secret Keys In Solving Problems For Others

**Each Wisdom Product may be purchased separately if so desired.

THE WISDOM CENTER
4051 Denton Highway • Fort Worth, TX 76117
1-817-759-BOOK
1-817-759-0300

You Will Love Our Website...!
TheWisdomCenter.tv   **K**

THE WISDOM BIBLE

Partnership Edit...

Over 120 Wisdom Study Guides Included Such As:

- ▶ *10 Qualities Of Uncommon Achievers*
- ▶ *18 Facts You Should Know About The Anointing*
- ▶ *21 Facts To Help You Identify Those Assigned To You*
- ▶ *31 Facts You Should Know About Your Assignment*
- ▶ *8 Keys That Unlock Victory In Every Attack*
- ▶ *22 Defense Techniques To Remember During Seasons Of Personal Attack*
- ▶ *20 Wisdom Keys And Techniques To Remember During An Uncommon Battle*
- ▶ *11 Benefits You Can Expect From God*
- ▶ *31 Facts You Should Know About Favor*
- ▶ *The Covenant Of 58 Blessings*
- ▶ *7 Keys To Receiving Your Miracle*
- ▶ *16 Facts You Should Remember About Contentious People*
- ▶ *5 Facts Solomon Taught About Contracts*
- ▶ *7 Facts You Should Know About Conflict*
- ▶ *6 Steps That Can Unlock Your Self-Confidence*
- ▶ *And Much More!*

Your Partnership makes such a difference in The Wisdom Center Outreach Ministries. I wanted to place a Gift in your hand that could last a lifetime for you and your family...**The Wisdom Study Bible.**

40 Years of Personal Notes...this Partnership Edition Bible contains 160 pages of my Personal Study Notes...that could forever change your Bible Study of The Word of God. This **Partnership Edition...**is my personal **Gift of Appreciation** when you sow your Sponsorship Seed of $1,000 to help us complete The Prayer Center and TV Studio Complex. An Uncommon Seed Always Creates An Uncommon Harvest!

Mike

Thank you from my heart for your Seed of Obedience (Luke 6:38).

This Gift Of Appreciation Will Change Your Bible Study For The Rest Of Your Life.

The Wisdom Bible

THE WISDOM CENTER
4051 Denton Highway • Fort Worth, TX 76117

1-817-759-BOOK
1-817-759-0300

You Will Love Our Website...!
TheWisdomCenter.tv

M

Spirit Music

TS-59

Songs...

1. A Holy Place
2. Anything You Want
3. Everything Comes From You
4. Fill This Place With Your Presence
5. First Thing Every Morning
6. Holy Spirit, I Want To Hear You
7. Holy Spirit, Move Again
8. Holy Spirit, You Are Enough
9. I Don't Know What I Would Do Without You
10. I Let Go (Of Anything That Stops Me)
11. I'll Just Fall On You
12. I Love You, Holy Spirit
13. I'm Building My Life Around You
14. I'm Giving Myself To You
15. I'm In Love! I'm In Love!
16. I Need Water (Holy Spirit, You're My Well)
17. In The Secret Place

18. In Your Presence, I'm Always Changed
19. In Your Presence (Miracles Are Born)
20. I've Got To Live In Your Presence
21. I Want To Hear Your Voice
22. I Will Do Things Your Way
23. Just One Day At A Time
24. Meet Me In The Secret Place
25. More Than Ever Before
26. Nobody Else Does What You Do
27. No No Walls!
28. Nothing Else Matters Anymore (Since I've Been In The Presence Of You Lord)
29. Nowhere Else
30. Once Again You've Answered
31. Only A Fool Would Try (To Live Without You)
32. Take Me Now
33. Teach Me How To Please You

34. There's No Place I'd Rather
35. Thy Word Is All That Matter
36. When I Get In Your Presenc
37. You're The Best Thing (Tha Ever Happened To Me)
38. You Are Wonderful
39. You've Done It Once
40. You Keep Changing Me
41. You Satisfy

**Each Wisdom Product may be purchased separately if so desired.*

 THE WISDOM CENTER 1-817-759-BOOK
4051 Denton Highway • Fort Worth, TX 76117   1-817-759-0300

You Will Love Our Website...!
TheWisdomCenter.tv

YOUR ASSIGNMENT IS YOUR DISTINCTION FROM OTHERS.

THE ASSIGNMENT: THE DREAM & THE DESTINY — MIKE MURDOCK

THE ASSIGNMENT: THE ANOINTING & THE ADVERSITY — MIKE MURDOCK

THE ASSIGNMENT: THE TRIALS & THE TRIUMPHS — MIKE MURDOCK

THE ASSIGNMENT: THE PAIN & THE PASSION — MIKE MURDOCK

Assignment 4 Book Pak!

Uncommon Wisdom For Discovering Your Life Assignment.

1 The Dream & The Destiny
Vol 1/<u>Book</u> (164 pg/B-74/$10)

2 The Anointing & The Adversity
Vol 2/<u>Book</u> (192 pg/B-75/$10)

3 The Trials & The Triumphs
Vol 3/<u>Book</u> (160 pg/B-97/$10)

4 The Pain & The Passion
Vol 4/<u>Book</u> (144 pg/B-98/$10)

**Each Wisdom Book may be purchased separately if so desired.

Buy 3 Books & Get The 4th Book Free!

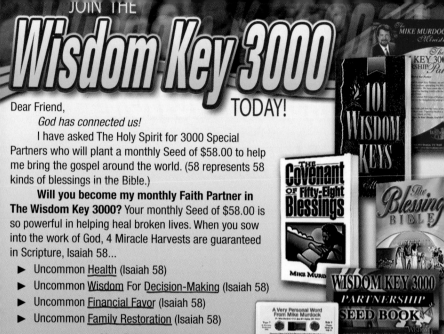

JOIN THE
Wisdom Key 3000
TODAY!

Dear Friend,

God has connected us!

I have asked The Holy Spirit for 3000 Special Partners who will plant a monthly Seed of $58.00 to help me bring the gospel around the world. (58 represents 58 kinds of blessings in the Bible.)

Will you become my monthly Faith Partner in The Wisdom Key 3000? Your monthly Seed of $58.00 is so powerful in helping heal broken lives. When you sow into the work of God, 4 Miracle Harvests are guaranteed in Scripture, Isaiah 58...

▶ Uncommon <u>Health</u> (Isaiah 58)
▶ Uncommon <u>Wisdom</u> For <u>Decision-Making</u> (Isaiah 58)
▶ Uncommon <u>Financial Favor</u> (Isaiah 58)
▶ Uncommon <u>Family Restoration</u> (Isaiah 58)

Your Faith Partner,

Mike Murdock

P.S. Please clip the coupon attached and return it to me today, so I can rush the Wisdom Key Partnership Pak to you...or call me at 1-817-759-0300.

PP-03
